# The Danish Christmas Cookbook

Marit Peters

# Contents

# INTRODUCTION

Christmas is a popular holiday in Denmark. Many aspects of the Danish Christmas are similar to other nations' celebrations and particularly those of other northern European nations. Denmark has Santa Claus in the guise of Julemanden – The Christmas Man and Christmas trees. The main Christmas dinner and gift giving is on Christmas Eve – December 24th. Denmark's Nordic cold climate, love of cosiness and stylish Scandinavian design creates a traditional festive atmosphere.

Denmark has some special traditions and Christmas foods of its own. For example Christmas Lunches are held by friends, families, schools and clubs where food and drink is consumed all day.

Danish Christmas food consists of hearty dishes such as roast duck, crispy roast pork, numerous pickled herring dishes, fried sausages and meatballs, vegetable dishes such as potatoes with sugar and many wonderful cookies and desserts.

Find out more about Danish Christmas food and traditions in this book.

# Remoulade

**Ingredients**

1 grated carrot
half a grated apple
half a finely chopped red onion
1 teaspoon of curry powder
3 tablespoons of sour cream
4 tablespoons of mayonnaise
1 teaspoon of wet mustard
2 finely chopped dill pickles
1 teaspoon of sugar
lemon juice
salt
pepper

Squeeze the carrot, apple, onion and pickle in a cloth to get rid of excess moisture.

Put the sour cream, mustard, mayonnaise, lemon juice and vegetables in a bowl and mix. Add the curry powder and mix. Add some salt and pepper, some lemon juice and the sugar. Mix.

Store in the refrigerator.

# Pickled Beetroot

**Ingredients**

1.5 kg/3.3 lb of cleaned beetroot
1 tablespoon of peppercorns
4 sprigs of thyme
peeled horseradish slices
850ml/3 and a half cups of white vinegar
600g/1.3 lb of caster sugar


Put the beetroot in a pan of water. Bring to the boil then cook for 50 minutes - until cooked.

Drain the beetroot then put in cod water for 5 minutes. Remove the beetroot skin. cut the beetroot into slices.

Mix the peppercorns, vinegar, sugar and thyme is a pan. Boil then add the beetroot and cook on a low heat for 5 minutes.

Put the beetroot sterilised jars with the liquid and a horseradish slice (one per jar). Put the lid on the jar and leave for a few weeks before using.

# Yellow Pea Soup

**Ingredients**

725g /1.6 lb of salt pork
400g/14 oz of dried yellow peas soaked in water for about 13 hours
3 peeled and chopped carrots
1 peeled and chopped leek
1 teaspoon dried parsley
1 bay leaf
240ml/1 cup of pork stock


Put the peas in a pan of water and bring to the boil. Cover and simmer for 20 minutes - until cooked.

Drain the peas.

In another pan, add the pork, pork stock, bay leaf, parsley, carrots and leeks. Simmer for 25 minutes. Drain, reserving the liquid.  Put the pork on a plate and cut it into pieces.

Put the peas in a pan with the liquid from the other pan. Serve the pork with the soup.

# Brown Gravy

**Ingredients**

5 tablespoons of butter
4 tablespoons of flour
5 tablespoons of sherry
4 tablespoons of white vinegar
940ml/4 cups of beef stock
salt
black pepper

Put the butter in a pan and melt on a low heat. Add the flour and make a paste. Add the stock and vinegar and stir to make a smooth mix.

Cook on a low heat for 6 minutes. Add some salt and pepper and stir. Cook on a low heat for 12 minutes. Add the sherry 2 minutes before the end of the cooking time.

# Potato Soup

**Ingredients**

2 peeled and chopped potatoes
1 ham bone
5 chopped spring onions/scallions
2 chopped stalks of celery
190g/6.7 oz of chopped cabbage
1 chopped carrot
2 tablespoons of flour
230ml/7.7 fl oz of cream
nutmeg


Put the ham bone in a pan with about 2 litres/ 8 cups of water. Bring to the boil then cook on a low heat for 1 hour 10 minutes.

Remove the meat from the ham bone and chop up. Put the potatoes, spring onions, celery, carrots, cabbage and ham in the pan. Boil then cover and cook on a low heat for 35 minutes.

Mix the flour with some water to make a paste. Add the soup and boil stirring constantly. Take off the heat and mix in the cream.

Serve with some nutmeg on top.

# Italian Salad

**Ingredients**

2 peeled carrots cut into cubes
85g/3 oz of frozen peas
7 asparagus spears cut into strips
2 tablespoons of mayonnaise
2 tablespoons of sour cream
2 teaspoons of Dijon mustard
salt
black pepper


Put the carrot in a pan of boiling water. Cook for 5 minutes -
until cooked. Remove and drain the carrots.

Add the asparagus to the water and cook for 3 minutes -
again until cooked.

Put the peas in the water and cook for a minute, then drain
the peas.

Mix the mustard, sour cream and mayonnaise in a bowl. Mix
in the peas, carrot and asparagus. Add some salt and pepper.

# Horseradish Sauce

**Ingredients**

3 tablespoons of grated horseradish
150ml/5 fl oz of sour cream
pinch of salt
2 tablespoons of sugar


Mix the ingredients in a bowl. Serve chilled.

# Kale Soup

## Ingredients

*soup*

150g/5 oz of cooked ham cubed
368g/13 oz of peeled and cubed potatoes
2 sliced carrots
2 chopped leeks
1 stick of chopped celery
1 finely chopped clove of garlic
210g/7.4 oz of chopped kale
sprig of thyme
1.4 litres/6 cups of chicken stock/broth
flour
black pepper

*broth*

453g/1 lb of ham hocks
1 carrot chopped in to four pieces
1 stick of celery cut in half
half an onion chopped into two pieces
2 bay leaves
1 clove of chopped garlic
1 sprig of thyme
1.6 litres/7 cups of water


To make the broth put the ingredients in a pan. Boil then cover and simmer for 3 hours. Strain the broth keeping the liquid.

For the soup, put the broth, ham, carrot, leek, celery, potatoes, garlic and pepper in a pan. Cook on a low heat for 1 and a half hours.

Add the kale and thyme. Cook for another 1 hour - until kale is cooked.

Stir in some flour and add some salt and pepper 30 minutes before the end of cooking.

# Apple Wedges

**Ingredients**

butter
apple wedges
almonds


Melt some butter in a pan. Add the apples and almonds and cook over a medium heat for 8 minutes - until golden. Serve with meat.

# Potato Salad

**Ingredients**

900g/2 lb of small potatoes
50g/1 cup of chopped chives
15g/half a cup of chopped parsley
1 tablespoon of capers
2 tablespoons of white vinegar
240ml/half a cup of oil
1 tablespoon of sour cream
salt
pepper

Put the potatoes in boiling salted water, boil, then cover and simmer for 15 minutes - until cooked. Drain and when cooled cut in slices.

Whisk the mustard, vinegar and oil in a bowl. Add the chives, capers, parsley and some salt and pepper and mix. Add the potatoes and mix.

# Dill and Mustard Sauce

**Ingredients**

4 tablespoons of chopped dill
3 tablespoons of Dijon mustard
1 and a half tablespoons of mayonnaise
1 tablespoon of honey
8 tablespoons of oil
3 tablespoons of white vinegar
salt
pepper


Put the mayonnaise, mustard, vinegar and honey in a bowl. Add the oil and whisk. Add the dill and some salt and pepper and stir.

This sauce is perfect for fish.

# Liver Pate

**Ingredients**

460g/1 lb of chicken livers
2 eggs
1 chopped onion
200ml/6.7 fl oz of whipping cream
2 tablespoons of butter
2 tablespoons of flour
pinch of nutmeg
salt
pepper


In a bowl, mix the flour with a little water and make a paste

Mix the flour, chicken livers, onion, eggs, butter, cream and some salt, black pepper and nutmeg in a bowl using a food processor to make a smooth mix.

Put the mix into pans and place in a baking dish filled with water. Put foil over the top and bake in a preheated oven at 200C/390F for 30 minutes. Remove the foil and cook for 25 minutes.

When cooled, Put in a covered plastic dish and store in the refrigerator.

# Danish Christmas Facts

The Danish word for Christmas is Jul. The word comes from Jol, which was a pre-Christmas celebration on the coldest full moon of the year.

Christmas markets are a feature of the festive season in Denmark. One famous market is that held at Tivoli Gardens in Copenhagen.

Real Christmas trees are often used in Denmark. Special trains are taken to the forest to cut down a tree.

Danes spend 25th and 26th December with friends and family. A traditional dinner on these days is herring and curry sauce (karrysild) and apple porridge with pork (aebleflaesk).

Cut and Paste Day – Klippeklistredag – is a day where schools and families make Christmas decorations.

Popular Danish Christmas decorations are Julehjerter - Christmas Hearts; Julesjerner - Christmas Stars; and julepynter - Christmas ornaments. These decorations are made from paper.

Popular flowers for Christmas in Denmark are Hyacinth and Amaryllis which are grown from bulbs in pots.

# Lingonberry Gravy

**Ingredients**

250ml/1 cup of red wine
1 tablespoons of lingonberry jam
500ml/2 cups of chicken stock/broth


Put the jam and wine in a pan and bring to the boil. Boil for 8 minutes. Add the stock and cook on a low heat for 15 minutes,

# Red Cabbage

## Ingredients

1 large shredded red cabbage
160ml/5.4 fl oz of white vinegar
180ml/6 fl oz of cranberry juice
160g/5.6 oz of sugar
salt
3 tablespoons of butter


Put the butter in a pot. Add the cabbage and cook on a medium heat for 6 minutes. Add the vinegar, sugar and cranberry juice and some salt.

Cover the pot and cook on a low heat for 70 minutes.

# White Cabbage with Cream

**Ingredients**

1 shredded white cabbage
4 tablespoons of butter
6 tablespoons of double cream
salt
pepper
nutmeg


Put the cabbage in a pan of boiling and cook for 7 minutes - until cooked. Drain.

Put the cabbage in a pan with the butter, cream and some salt pepper and nutmeg. Stir and cook for 2 minutes.

**Christmas Cookies  (Pebernoder)**

**Oat Balls**

# Cucumber Salad



**Ingredients**

3 cucumbers peeled ad cut into thin slices
240ml/1 cup of water
240ml/1 cup of white vinegar
4 tablespoons of sugar
black pepper
salt

Put the cucumber in a bowl and sprinkle with some salt.
Leave for 10 minutes.

Drain the cucumber slices.

Mix the vinegar, water, sugar and pepper. Put the mix in a
bowl with the cucumers. Put in the refrigerator for 2 hours.

Drain before serving.

# Caramel Potatoes

**Ingredients**

800g/1.7 lb of small potatoes
140g/5 oz of white sugar
70g/2.5 oz of butter


Put the potatoes in boiling salted water. Boil until cooked.

Drain the potatoes and place in cold water. Drain again and take the skin off. Leave to cool.

Put the sugar in a pan and melt to make a liquid. Add the butter and cook for 4 minutes.

Add the potatoes and cook on a medium heat for 12 minutes stirring occasionally.

# Hasselback Potatoes

**Ingredients**



1 kg/2.2 lb of small potatoes
45g/1.5 oz of melted butter
3 tablespoons of olive oil
chopped fresh dill

Slice the potatoes, but do not fully cut them. Put on a baking tray. Coat with the butter, olive oil and dill. Cook in a preheated oven at 200C/392C for 1 hour and 10 minutes - until cooked and crispy.

# Curried Herring

**Ingredients**

450g/1 lb of pickled herring (drained if from a jar) cut into chunks
1 finely chopped onion
1 finely chopped small onion
1 tablespoon of chopped capers
chopped chives
1 tablespoon of curry powder (mild)
80ml/1 third of a cup of mayonnaise
80ml/1 third of a cup of sour cream
olive oil
salt


Cook the onion in some oil in a pan for 6 minutes. Add a little salt and the curry powder and mix. Cook for 2 minutes. Remove from the heat.

Put the herring, sour cream, capers, mayonnaise, apple and chives in a bowl and mix. Add the onion and some salt and mix. Serve on rye bread.

# Poached Cod

**Ingredients**

4 frozen cod fillets
2 tablespoons of honey
2 tablespoons of salt
6 black peppercorns
6 tablespoons of melted butter
3 bay leaves
salt


Mix the honey with 500ml/2 cups of hot water and add a little salt.

Put the fish in a pan. Add the honey mix. Add some more water to cover the cod. Add the bay leaves and peppercorns. Bring to the boil then cook on a low heat for 7 minutes.

Remove the fish and dry using a paper towel. Put on a baking sheet and add the butter and a little salt. Grill/broil for 4 minutes.

# Danish Christmas Facts

The main Christmas meal in Denmark is eaten on December 24th.

A traditional Christmas meal in Denmark on December 24th is roast duck, roast pork (flæskesteg) with brown gravy, caramel potatoes, boiled potatoes and red cabbage. Dessert rice pudding with cheery sauce - Ris a l'Amande.

Father Christmas is called Julemanden in Danish. This is translated as The Christmas Man. He is helped during Christmas by a group of Elves called Nisser. Children leave rice pudding, saucers of milk and other foods for them on the afternoon of the 24th December. Julemanden delivers presents on the 24th December dressed in red robes driving a sleigh with reindeer.

On December 13th Santa Lucia comes to Denmark to bring light. She dresses in white. On this day children take part in a Santa Lucia parade dressed in white robes.

In Denmark a Christmas calendar television series - Julekalender - containing 24 episodes is shown in December. Several Danish channels have their own series.

When rice pudding is eaten on December 24 a blanched almond is in the rice pudding. Whoever finds it gets a prize which traditionally is a marzipan pig but can also be a toy

# Herring With Mustard

**Ingredients**



350g/12 oz of pickled herring (drained if from a jar) cut into chunks
120m/4 fl oz of sour cream
5 tablespoons of mayonnaise
1 finely chopped red onion
1 tablespoon of chopped fresh dill
2 tablespoons of Dijon mustard
3 tablespoons of sweet mustard
1 teaspoon of sugar
1 tablespoon of chopped capers
salt
pepper


Mix the sour cream, mayonnaise and mustard in a bowl. Add the onion, dill, capers, sugar and some salt and pepper.

Add the herring and mix.

Rye Bread

Open Faced Sandwiches

# Poached Cod

**Ingredients**

750g/1 and a half lb of of skinned and boned cod fillets
110g/4 oz of bacon
oil
1 litre of water
salt


Boil the water and a little sat in a pan. Add the cod and boil.
Cook on a low heat for 12 minutes - until cooked. Drain the
fish.

Fry the bacon in some oil until crispy.

Serve the cod with Dill and Mustard Sauce and the bacon.

# Fried Plaice Fillet

**Ingredients**

2 plaice fillets
1 egg
118ml/half a cup of milk
60g/half a cup of flour
60g/half a cup of dried breadcrumbs
butter
vegetable oil
salt
black pepper
lemon slices


Mix the flour with some salt.

Put the fillets in the milk, then the flour  and then the breadcrumbs.

Heat some butter and oil on a pan. Fry the fillets for 3 minutes in each side - until golden brown. Serve with lemon slices.

# Oysters with Horseradish and Apple



**Ingredients**

16 shucked oysters
2 tablespoons of white wine vinegar
1 tablespoon of finely chopped shallot
half a teaspoon of honey
vegetable oil
2 tablespoons of finely chopped green apple
1 tablespoon of grated horseradish
fresh dill
white pepper


Mix the shallot, vinegar, honey, dill, apple, horseradish and some white pepper in a bowl. Leave for 30 minutes.

Put the oysters in their shells and place on some ice. Top with the dressing and a little dill.

# Herring Salad

## Ingredients

198g/7 oz of chopped pickled herring fillets
450g/1 lb of sliced pickled beetroot
1 chopped green apple
420g/15 oz of cooked peeled potato
half a cup of chopped dill pickle
1 finely chopped onion
some liquid from the pickled beetroot


Put the ingredients in a bowl and mix. Cover and refrigerate
for 2 days.

# Fishcakes

**Ingredients**

450g/1 lb of chopped white fish with no skin or bones
80ml/2.7 fl oz of heavy cream
a quarter of a finely chopped onion
chopped fresh parsley
chopped fresh dill
1 teaspoon of lemon zest
30g/a quarter cup of flour
1 egg
salt
black pepper
oil
butter

Mix the fish, egg, onion, cream, flour, lemon zest with some parsley, dill and salt and pepper in a food processor to make a slightly chunky mix.

Put the mix in the refrigerator for 45 minutes.

Form into 12 patties and fry in a mixture of oil and butter on both sides until the fish is cooked.

# Apple Porridge with Pork

**Ingredients**

16 salted pork belly slices
8 green tart apples cut into segments
2 tablespoons of sugar
1 teaspoon of chopped fresh thyme
salt
pepper
rye bread


Put the pork in a pan and cook on each side until crispy. Put the pork on a plate.

Put the apples, thyme, 240ml/half a cup of water and sugar in the pan the pork was cooked in. Cover and cook for 15 minutes until the apples have softened. Add some salt and pepper.

Serve the apple porridge and pork on slices of rye bread.

# Chicken Salad

**Ingredients**

750g/1 and a half lb of chicken fillets
1 carrot
1 onion chopped into 4 pieces
230g/8 oz of sliced mushrooms.
2 bay leaves
240ml/1 cup of sour cream
1 teaspoon of Dijon mustard
salt
pepper
1 tablespoon of curry powder
oil


Put the chicken, bay leaves, onion and carrot in a pan of boiling water. Cook on a low heat for 8 minutes - until the chicken is cooked. Reserve the chicken and cut into chunks.

Fry the mushrooms in some oil.

Mix the chicken and mushrooms with the rest of the ingredients and some salt and pepper in a bowl.

# Danish Christmas Facts

After Christmas dinner on December 24th Danes join hands and walk around the Christmas tree singing Christmas hymns. Then the presents are opened.

Baking cookies and cakes is a popular Christmas activity in Denmark.

The Christmas Church service on Christmas Eve is at 4 pm before Christmas dinner.

A Danish tradition on Christmas Eve is to give animals a treat. For example people go for a walk and feed the birds.

The tradition of the Christmas tree was started in the 19th century and inspired by Germany.

December 23rd is called Little Yule Eve in Denmark. Rice pudding is made and served with brown sugar, butter and cinnamon. This same pudding is eaten on 24th with cherry sauce.

Danish homed often have an advent candle – kalenderlys. This has December 1-24 written on it vertically. It is burnt every day until the line of the next day.

# Chicken and Asparagus Tarts

**Ingredients**

450g/1 lb of chicken fillets
200g/7 oz of asparagus
1 carrot
1 onion
fresh dill
7 tablespoons of flour
individual savoury tart cases
50g/1.7 oz of butter
250ml/1 cup of milk
2 litres/8 and a half cups of water
1 chicken stock cube
salt
black pepper

Put the asparagus in a pan of boiling water and cook for 3 minutes. Drain and chop the asparagus.

Boil the water. Add the stock cube. Add the chicken, onion, carrot, some dill and some salt and pepper. Bring to a boil again then cover and cook on a low heat for about 20 minutes - until cooked.

Take the chicken out and chop. Reserve 250ml/1 cup of the cooking liquid.

Put the butter in a pan and melt. Add the flour and make a

paste. Add the milk and 250ml/1 cup of cooking liquid. Whist all the time and cook to get rid of any lumps. Cook on a low heat for 7 minutes until thick.

Add the asparagus and chicken and heat for 8 minutes. Put the mix in the tart cases.

Meatballs in Curry Sauce

Roast Pork with Red Cabbage and Caramel Potatoes

# Meatballs with Curry Sauce

**Ingredients**

255g/9 oz of minced/ground pork
255g/9 oz of minced/ground beef
milk
a quarter of chopped onion
1 egg
55g/a quarter cup of breadcrumbs
60ml/a quarter cup of carbonated water
55g/a quarter cup of flour
salt
black pepper

*sauce*

1 finely chopped onion
3 teaspoons of curry powder
1 chopped apple
2 tablespoons of flour
650ml/2 and 3 quarter cups of meatball cooking water
oil

Mix the meat. Add the milk, egg and onion and mix. Stir in the breadcrumbs, flour, water, and some salt and pepper. Place in the refrigerator for 30 minutes.

Make egg shaped balls from the mix. Put the meatballs in a pan of hot water and boil for 15 minutes. Drain them.

Reserve the liquid.

For the curry sauce, fry the onions in some oil for 2 minutes. Add the curry powder and cook for 2 minutes, Add the apple and fry for 2 minutes,. Add the flour and mix. Add the water and cook on a low heat for 15 minutes.

Add the meatballs to the curry sauce and cook for 6 minutes to warm up.

# Parisian Steak

**Ingredients**

7 oz/200g of ground/minced beef
half a chopped red onion
2 tablespoons of chopped pickled beetroot
4 slices of thick white bread
3 tablespoons of fresh horseradish
1 egg
1 teaspoon of Dijon mustard
1 teaspoon of chopped capers
salt
pepper

Mix the meat, mustard, capers, egg and some salt and pepper together. Make into four patties.

Put the each patty on a slice of bread. Fry in butter meat side down until browned. Turn over and fry on bread side down.

Put each patty on a plate bread side down. Top with some of the onion, beetroot and fresh horseradish.

# Roast Pork

**Ingredients**

1 kg/2.2 lb of pork joint (boneless)
sliced onion
sliced carrot
sea salt


Cut grooves in the pork skin. Rub the pork with the salt.

Put on a rack and place the rack in a roasting tin. Add 500ml/2 cups of water and the onion and carrot.

Cook in a preheated oven at 225C/440F for 20 minutes. Cook for 1 hour and 25 minutes at 200C/400F.

Leave the pork for 20 minutes before slicing.

# Roast Turkey With Juniper Stuffing

**Ingredients**

1 turkey
2 onions cut into quarters
1 orange cut into quarters
butter
2 chopped carrots
parsley

*stuffing*

butter
1 tablespoon of crushed juniper berries
2 chopped onions
2 chopped cloves of garlic
1 chopped stick of celery
250g/8.8 oz of white breadcrumbs
50g/1.7 oz of dried cranberries
1 teaspoon of orange zest
chopped parsley
2 beaten eggs

salt
pepper

Put one onion and the orange in the turkey. Rub butter over the turkey. Add some salt and pepper.

For the stuffing, melt some butter in a pan and add the garlic and onions and fry for 15 minutes.

Add the juniper. Take off the heat and add the breadcrumbs, cranberries, zest, apple. eggs and some parsley.  Butter a baking tray and put the stuffing in it. Bake the stuffing for 30 minutes.

Put the rest of the onion and the carrot on a roasting pan. Put the turkey on top. cover with foil and bake in a preheated oven at 180C/356F. Allow about 45 minutes cooking time  for each 1kg/2.2 lbs of turkey.

Serve with the stuffing.

# Danish Christmas Facts

During the Christmas period Christmas lunches are held. The lunch is called Juleforkost (Yule Lunch) in Danish. Family yule lunches (familiejulefrokost) are also held. The lunches last throughout the day and are held at work places, schools and clubs and by groups of friends and families.

A typical Yule Lunch menu is:

First course is seafood such as open face sandwiches with shrimp, pickled herring, smoked salmon and deep fried plaice with remoulade.

Next are meats such as fried sausages, meatballs, liver pate, boiled ham and fried pork. The meats are served with cabbage.

The dessert course includes cheese, clementines and oranges.

The lunch is accompanied by beer and schnapps.

Danish Christmas decorations tend to be quite minimalist and inspired by nature with lots of decorations made from pine and candles. Colours used are silver, white green and red.

Marzipan sweets and chocolates are very popular during the Christmas period in Denmark.

# Mashed Potatoes With Bacon and Onions

## Ingredients

1 kg/2.2 lb of potatoes
4 finely chopped rashers of bacon
1 sliced onion
90ml/3 fl oz of milk
1 tablespoon of butter
3 tablespoons of sour cream
oil
salt
pepper
ground nutmeg


Put the potatoes in a pan of water and bring to the boil. Cover and cook on a low heat for 15 minutes - until cooked. Drain.

Put the butter and milk in a pan and heat for 6 minutes.

Fry the potatoes and bacon in some oil in a pan until crispy.

Put the potatoes in a bowl and add the milk mix. Mash or blend the potatoes. Add the sour cream and mix. Add some salt and pepper.

Serve the mashed potato topped with a little nutmeg and some onions and bacon.

# Beef Patties
# With Cream Sauce

**Ingredients**

750g/1.6 lb of minced/ground beef
3 sliced onions
parsley
300ml/1 and a quarter cups of beef stock/broth
cornflour/cornstarch
450m/15 fl oz of whipping cream
salt
pepper
oil
butter


Fry the onion in some oil for 15 minimizes - until crispy.

Make patties put of the beef and add some salt and pepper. Fry them in a mixture of butter and oil on a medium heat in a pan for 8 minutes on each side. Take the patties out of the pan.

Mix the stock/broth in a bowl with a little cornflour. Add to the frying pan and simmer for 7 minutes - until the liquid thickens. Add the cream and cook for 4 minutes.

Serve the patties  with the sauce and garnish with parsley.

# Roast Duck

## Ingredients

1 duck
1 green apple cut into four
2 red onions cut into four
239g/8.4 oz of chopped destoned prunes
6 tablespoons of orange juice
2 bay leaves
3 sprigs of thyme
salt
pepper

Mix the onion, apple, prunes, bay leaves, thyme and orange juice in a bowl with some salt and pepper.

Rub salt on the duck - on the outside and in the cavity. Stuff the duck with the other mix. Close the duck.

Put on a rack in a baking pan. Add 1 litre/4 cups of water to the pan. Put the duck on the rack. Roast in a preheated oven at 165C/330F for 3 hours - until cooked.

# Open Faced Sandwich

**Ingredients**

slices of rye bread - such as Danish rugbrød

*toppings include:*

pickled herring
thinly sliced cheese
tomato slices
boiled egg slices
pork liver pate
bacon
sliced radish
fried mushrooms
horseradish
boiled egg slices
fried onion
tomato slices
chives
cress
shrimp
meat slices, cold cuts, pieces of meat
smoked salmon
caviar
mackerel in tomato sauce
red onion slices
Italian Salad (mayonnaise with peas, sliced carrot and sliced boiled asparagus)

The bread is buttered. On some occasions lard is used

Typical open sandwich combinations include:

smoked eel with scrambled egg and sliced radish

liver pate with bacon and mushrooms

roast beef with remoulade and horseradish

roast pork with cabbage and pickles

boiled egg slices with prawns, mayonnaise and tomato slices
steamed fish, battered fish, shrimp, caviar and mayonnaise

# Christmas Cookies

**Ingredients**

180g/1 and a half cups of flour
1 egg
120g/half a cup of butter
100g/half a cup of sugar
ground cardamon
ground cinnamon


Mix the butter and sugar to make a smooth mix. Add the egg flour, and some cardamon and cinnamon. Mix well, then add the butter and sugar mix and make a smooth mix.

Make into 3 balls, then make strings from them. Cut into pieces. Put in a baking tray.

Bake in a preheated oven at 176C/350F for 12 minutes.

**Paris Beef**

**Apple Porridge with Pork**

# Fruit Salad

## Ingredients

300ml/1 and a quarter cups of whipped cream
3 sliced bananas
1 chopped apple
4 mandarins cut into segments
10 grapes cut in half
40g/1.4 oz of marzipan cut into chunks
2 tablespoons of chopped dark chocolate


Put the fruit, chocolate and marzipan in a bowl. Whip the
cream and add to the rest of the ingredients.

# Carrot Bread Rolls

**Ingredients**

270g/9 and a half oz of grated carrots
85g/3 oz of sunflower seeds
1.1 kg/2.4 lb of flour
55g/2 oz of yeast
600ml/2 and a half cups of warm water
2 teaspoons of sugar
3 tablespoons of oil
half a teaspoon of salt
1 beaten egg
extra sunflower seeds

Mix the yeast with a little of the warm water. Leave for 8 minutes. Add the rest of the ingredients to the yeast and mix to make a dough. Cover the bowl with a damp towel and leave in a warm place for 1 hour.

Separate into pieces - about 25 - and toll into bun shapes. Put on a baking sheet covered with parchment/baking papers. Leave for 35 minutes in a warm place to rise.

Brush the rolls with beaten eggs and top with some sunflower seeds.

Cook in a preheated oven at 220C/428F for 22 minutes.

# Rice Pudding

## Ingredients

600ml/2 and a half cups of whipped double/heavy cream
160g/5.6 oz of almonds
2 tablespoons of sugar
seeds from 2 vanilla pods
salt


Bring the milk and rice to the boil stirring all the time.  Add some salt. Cook on a low heat for 35 minutes stirring numerous times. refrigerate for 10 hours before serving.

Soak the almonds in hot water for 12 minutes. Remove the skins and chop. Reserve one whole almond.

Mix the vanilla seeds with the sugar.

Add the vanilla and sugar mix and almonds to the cream. Add to the porridge. Put the almond in the rice porridge.

Refrigerate before serving. Serve with cherry sauce.

# Cherry Sauce

**Ingredients**



600g/1.3 lb of cherries with the seeds taken out
110g/3.8 oz of sugar
1 stick of cinnamon
sees from one vanilla pod
2 tablespoons of arrowroot flour/powder


Put the cherries, sugar, vanilla and cinnamon in a pan and cover with water. Bring to the boil and cook until the sugar has dissolved. Cook on a low heat for 4 minutes. Mix the arrowroot with a little water to make a paste. Add to the mix then cook on a low heat for 3 minutes and stir.

Serve cool with Rice Pudding.

# Apple Pudding

**Ingredients**

whipped Cream
grated apple
crushed cookies


Put some crushed cookies in a glass. Add some grated apple and top with whipped cream.

# Jewish Cookies

**Ingredients**

*dough*

140g/5 oz of butter
1 egg
240g/8.5 oz of flour
90g/3.7 oz of sugar

*topping*

4 tablespoons of chopped almonds
1 egg
3 tablespoons of sugar
1 tablespoon of cinnamon


For the dough, mix the flour and butter to make a crumble type mix. Add the sugar and egg and mix to make the dough.

Put the dough in a bowl, cover with plastic wrap and put in the fridge for 35 minutes.

Roll out the dough. Cut into quite small cookie shapes. Put on a baking tray lined with baking/parchment paper. Top with some beaten egg.

Mix the topping ingredients in a bowl. Put on top of the cookies. Cook in a preheated oven at 200C/400F for 8 minutes.

# Pancake Balls

**Ingredients**

250g/2 cups of flour
1 tablespoon of white sugar
2 egg whites
2 egg yolks
3 tablespoons of melted butter
pinch of bicarbonate of soda/baking soda
half a tablespoon of baking powder
500ml/2 cups of buttermilk
salt
oil


Mix the egg white to make a stiff mix.

Mix the flour, egg yolks, melted butter, sugar, bicarbonate of soda, baking powder and some salt in a bowl and make a smooth mix. Gently sir in the egg whites.

These are traditionally cooked in a special pan called an Aebleskiver pan which has small holes for the pancakes. A drop of oil is placed in the holes followed by 2 tablespoons of the pancake batter. Cook the pancake puffs turning frequently until cooked.

An alternative method of cooking is using egg ramekins on a baking sheet in a medium oven.

Pancake Balls (Aebleskiver)

Rice Pudding With Cinnamon, Sugar and Butter

# Goose Bread Cake

**Ingredients**

70g /2.4 oz of puff pastry
2 leaves of gelatine/gelatin
200ml of whipping cream
1 vanilla pod with the seeds removed
4 teaspoons of icing/confectioners' sugar
150g/5.3 oz of plum jam
120g/4.2 oz of marzipan
melted dark chocolate
2 tablespoons of cornflour/cornstarch

Roll out the puff pastry sheets. Put in a baking sheet and bake on a preheated oven at 190C for 10 minutes.  Leave them to cool.

Put the gelatine in cold water and leave for 10 minutes. Drain off the excess water.

Put half the cream in a pan and heat gently stirring in the cornflour.  Add the gelatine and mix and warm until melted. Let the mix cool a little.

Put the rest of the cream in a bowl with the sugar and vanilla seeds.

Put a tablespoon of the cold cream in the warmed cream and mix. Mix the cold and warm cream mixtures then refrigerate for 2 hours.

Spread plum jam on the puff pastry. Spread the cream on top and form into a pyramid type shape.

Place in the freezer (in a freezer bag) for 6 hours.

Roll out the marzipan and drape on top keeping a curved pyramid type shape.

Drizzle over melted chocolate. Cut into slices.

# Ginger Cookies

**Ingredients**

60g/2.1 oz of chopped deskinned almonds
140g/5 oz of butter
70g/2.5 oz of syrup
140g/5 oz of brown sugar
2 teaspoons of cinnamon
2 teaspoons of ginger
1 crushed clove
1 tablespoon of orange juice
1 teaspoon of orange zest
1 teaspoon of bicarbonate of soda/baking soda


Put the butter, sugar and syrup in a pan. Boil then take off the heat. Leave to cool.

Mix the bicarbonate of soda with the orange juice and add to the sugar mix.

Mix the cinnamon, cloves, ginger, almonds, zest and flour in a bowl. Add to the sugar mix and make a dough.

Wrap the dough in clingfilm/plastic wrap and place in the refrigerator for 10 hours.

Roll out the dough and cut out cookie shapes. Put on a baking tray lined with parchment paper or grease and bake in a preheated oven at 180C/377F for 8 minutes.

# Oat Balls

**Ingredients**

6 tablespoons of butter
135g/1 and a half cups of oats
50g/a quarter cup of sugar
2 tablespoons of cocoa powder (unsweetened)
coconut flakes
drop of vanilla extract


Mix the butter, sugar, cocoa, vanilla extract and oats in a
bowl. Put in the refrigerator for 30 minutes. Roll into balls.
Roll in the coconut flakes. Put in the refrigerator for 1 hour.

# Marzipan

**Ingredients**

300g/10 oz of almonds
60ml/a quarter of a cup of water
70g/3 thirds of a cup of sugar


Soak the almonds in hot water for 6 minutes. Drain the almonds. Remove the almond skins.

Blend the almonds in a food processor to make a flour like mix.

Boil the sugar and water in a pan for 7 minutes. When a syrup is made leave to cool.

Put the syrup and almonds in a bowl. Mix to make a smooth dough.

Roll out the dough into a long tube type shape. Place in the refrigerator for 4 hours. Slice into portions.

# Citronfromage

**Ingredients**

1 tablespoon of lemon zest
3 egg yolks
3 egg whites
100g/3.5 oz of sugar
2 and a half teaspoons of gelatine/gelatin
120ml/half a cup of water
3 tablespoons of lemon juice
240ml/half a pint of whipped cream


Put the gelatin in the cold water in a bowl and leave for 10 minutes. Heat up a pan of water - make sure it is not boiling. Put the bowl with the gelatine over the pan and melt the gelatine.

Mix the egg yolks and sugar to make a smooth mix.

Mix the egg mix with the gelatine. Stir in the lemon juice. Put in the refrigerator for 3 hours.

Whisk the egg whites to make a paste.

Mix in the lemon zest and cream. Add the egg whites and stir.

# Candied Almonds

**Ingredients**

240g/2 cups of almonds
120ml/half a cup of water
3 teaspoons of cinnamon
200g/1 cup of sugar


Put the water, sugar and cinnamon in a pan Bring to a boil then add the almonds. Cook stirring all the time until the liquid has gone.

Put the almonds on some baking/parchment paper and leave to cool.

# Fried Cookies

**Ingredients**

440g/1 lb of butter
130g/4.5 oz of flour
half a teaspoon of bicarbonate of soda/baking soda
pinch of ground cardamon
1 teaspoon of lemon zest
40g/1.4 oz of sugar
icing/confectioners' sugar
1 egg
1 tablespoon of double/heavy cream
oil


Mix the flour, butter, bicarbonate of soda, sugar, cardamon and lemon zest in a bowl. Add the egg and cream and make a dough. Place the dough in the refrigerator for 4 hours.

Roll out the dough. Cut into small strips. Make a cut in then middle of a strip and pull one end of the dough strip through the hole. Repeat with each strip.

Fry in hot oil for a few minutes until golden. Drain them and dry on a towel. Add some icing sugar.

# Red Berry Pudding

**Ingredients**

600g/1.3 lb of chopped strawberries
130g/4.5 oz of caster/superfine sugar
120g/4.2 oz of raspberries
120g/4.2 oz of redcurrants
270ml/9 fl oz of water
heavy cream
1 and a half tablespoons of potato flour/starch

Put the strawberries in a pan with the sugar and water. Bring to the boil then cook on a low heat for 3 minutes. Remove from the heat and stir.

Mix the potato flour with a tablespoon of water and make a paste. Add to the fruit mix and cook the mix until it comes to the boil.

Put the mix in bowls/glasses. Put in the refrigerator for 2 hours. Serve with some cream on top.

# Kringle

**Ingredients**

*filling*

1 egg yolk
255g/9 oz of cream cheese
55g/2 oz of brown sugar
ground cinnamon
235g/1 cup of chopped toasted walnuts

*pastry*

300g/2 cups of flour
salt
230g/1 cup of butter cut into pieces
240ml/1 cup of sour cream

*glaze*

water
icing/confectioners' sugar


For the pastry, mix the salt and flour. Add the butter and mix well. Add the sour cream and make a dough. Put the dough in plastic wrap and place in the refrigerator for 10 hours.

For the filling mix the egg, sugar, cream cheese and some cinnamon to make a smooth mix, Add the walnuts.

Cut the dough into two pieces. Roll them into rectangular sheets. Put the filling in the centre strip of the dough sheets. Cut into 8 strips on the long side of each piece of dough. Fold the strips over the filling in the centre.

Put the dough on some parchment paper on a baking sheet. Cook in a preheated oven at 190C/375F for 30 minutes.

Mix together some confectioners' sugar and some water in a bowl and mix. Spoon over the kringle when cool.

# Mulled Wine

**Ingredients**

1 tablespoon of orange zest
2 sticks of cinnamon
8 cloves
4 cardamon pods
7 tablespoons of brown sugar
250ml/1 cup of water
90ml/3 fl oz of orange juice
800ml/2 and a half cups of wine


Put the water, sugar, orange zest, cinnamon, cloves and cardamon in a pan. Boil, then cook on a low heat for 30 minutes. Take out the orange zest, cinnamon and cloves before serving.

# Photo Credits

## Cover Picture

https://commons.wikimedia.org/wiki/File:Risalamande,_a_Danish_Christmas_dessert.jpg

25 December 2022

Lorie Shaull

## Christmas Hearts

https://commons.wikimedia.org/wiki/File:Julehjerter.jpg

27 December 2006

Jens Gyldenkærne Clausen

## Christmas Tree

https://commons.wikimedia.org/wiki/File:Christmas_tree_in_Copenhagen_(December_2017)_3.jpg

8 December 2017

Visem

## Christmas Cookies

https://commons.wikimedia.org/wiki/File:Spicy_little_ones_-_Pebbern%C3%B6dder.jpg

20 December 2009

Lene

## Oat Balls

https://commons.wikimedia.org/wiki/File:Havregrynskugle
r_2011-12-23.jpg

23 December 2011

Slaunger

## Rye Bread

https://commons.wikimedia.org/wiki/File:Rugbr
%C3%B8d.JPG

19 December 2005

Sten Porse

## Open Faced Sandwich

https://commons.wikimedia.org/wiki/File:Smoerrebroed.jp
g

21 April 2008

Vargklo~commonswiki

## Meatballs in Curry Sauce

https://commons.wikimedia.org/wiki/File:Boller_i_karry_med_ris_og_agurkesalat.jpg

December 2008

Nillerdk

## Roast Pork With Caramel Potatoes

https://commons.wikimedia.org/wiki/File:Fl%C3%A6skesteg_r%C3%B8dk%C3%A5l_brunede_kartofler.jpg

6 September 2008

Nillerdk

## Paris Beef

https://commons.wikimedia.org/wiki/File:Pariserb%C3%B8f_(5988859688).jpg

26 July 2011

cyclonebill

## Apple Porridge With Pork

https://commons.wikimedia.org/wiki/File:%C3%86blefl%C3%A6sk_2.jpg

21 November 2009

Nillerd


## Rice Pudding With Cinnamon, Sugar and Butter

https://commons.wikimedia.org/wiki/File:Risengr
%C3%B8d.jpg

12 November 2006

EPO


## Pancake Balls

https://commons.wikimedia.org/wiki/File:Aebleskiver1.jpg

4 November 200

Michael Meinecke